EDUCATION AND THE STATE.

BACCALAUREATE SERMON.

UNIVERSITY OF WISCONSIN.

JUNE, 17, 1877.

JOHN BASCOM.

BACCALAUREATE SERMON.

Prov. 4:7. Wisdom is the principal thing; therefore get wisdom: and with all thy getting, get understanding.

This injunction, which sprang three thousand years ago out of the best wisdom of that time, has been gathering clearness in the consciousness of all true men, in the consciousness of all progressive nations, ever since. Wisdom is our most comprehensive expression for excellence; our wise man is our best man. Science and religion both take it in at their point of intersection, and are both included by it. Wisdom remains the centre at which all knowledge and all virtue meet, and from which they take their departure. We mean by wisdom the knowledge which gives a mastery over physical forces, the insight which discloses the constructive laws of mind and society, and that living obedience which puts itself in perfect harmony with this innermost truth of things. This wisdom is for men and for States the principal thing. Accepting the proposition, Wisdom is the principal thing, we accept the corollary, and would obey the injuction: Get wisdom; and with all thy getting, get understanding.

The applicability of this precept to us in our collective capacity, the State, suggests our theme. We propose to discuss Education and the State. We thought at first of entitling our topic, Higher Education and the State; but further consideration made us unwilling to seem thus to divide knowledge, and to disintegrate discipline; and to assign a portion here and a portion there, to give one less and another more according to our notion of the wants of men. Wisdom is one, and is passing always into a higher and yet higher unity. . This wisdom it is, not arithmetic or geography, which is the principal thing; which we are to labor after, each of us according to our capacity. There is no more opportunity in education than in wisdom itself to divide acquisition into primary and higher, and to bid the State and so to bid the masses halt at the line of separation. All knowledge is for the sake of all knowledge, and is for all: and knowledge is so valuable because it gathers up fact and fact, relation and relation, in endless sequence. The community in its books, papers, discourses, discussions; in its arts, commerce and government, is the true school of the citizen; but it can remain this school only as there is poured into it freely from all quarters every available form of knowledge, from the lowest to the highest. These fountains of wisdom by the wayside, at which all are to drink, must be fed from large areas, near at hand and remote, from deep places and high places, from broad plateaus and far-reaching mountains, and so be made pure and perennial. The community is the school of the citizen, his abiding instructor; but that it may be this, constantly and wisely this, two things are necessary. All inquiry, all truth must be passed over to the community by school and college, by pulpit and press, as a common possession; and, as a supplement to this, every citizen must have the means of instruction so open to him that he shall be brought in living contact with this knowledge. In this process, by which enterprise and thought percolate the community as flowing waters, and come to the surface everywhere for every one as refreshing knowledge, higher schools, in all their grades, are of just as much moment as the most primary ones. We do not learn the alphabet for its own sake, but that we may climb by it into science, philosophy and literature. No more do we learn grammar and arithmetic for their sakes, but only as continuations of our lines of ascent into intellectual manhood. Good citizenship, intelligence, virtue are held as a living spirit in the entire nation, must be held and nourished in the nation, and be gotten by the individual from the nation. Our national life measures our national strength, and our national instruction measures our national life. There are here no bounds of knowledge, no divisions of advantage. The highest truths must be found in descent, as a beam of light, to the lowest social ranks; and from the lowest social ranks every clear eye must be directed upward, drinking in the radiance of the higher air.

Claiming, then, that our inheritance in wisdom is one of indivisible and inseparable portions, we ask, Is instruction a function of the State, a function which it ought to take up, and which it can discharge advantageously?

Nothing in government is absolute. Its functions, though lying in certain general directions, are changeable with circumstances. While we answer, therefore, our triple question on general principles, we wish also to answer it as modified by the existing condition of the Western States.

The first branch of our inquiry is, Is education a function of the State? A theory of government has sprung up, in reaction against the meddlesome, mistaken and tyrannical tendencies of the past, that the proper, the almost exclusive, province of civil government is protection. This view is much too narrow, not only for all experience hitherto, not only for the functions which governments are daily and beneficently exercising, but also for any sufficient estimate of their powers and duties. Government is the offspring of human wants; and needs, in its action, no other justification than that offered by a skillful and successful supply of those wants. Government may do all that it can advantageously do, advantageously do with a broad forecast of immediate and remote results. A good action in the State, as in the person, requires no other commendation than its goodness. The first portion of our question, therefore, Is education a function of the State? is answered in the affirmative, if the two remaining portions are so answered. If education is shown to be a demand which the State can meet, and one which is not likely to be well met without it, then the State has no occasion of hesitancy as to its right to do what it can do for the welfare of its citizens.

The first duty of a government is, indeed, the protection of its citizens in the free exercise of all their rights, but the second duty, and one for which in large part we perform the first duty, is to provide those common conditions of national growth which lie beyond the reach of individual and corporate action. In fulfillment of this obligation, governments construct roads, establish postal systems, open harbors, erect light-houses, make internal improvements, and provide all needful conditions of national activity. A government cannot hesitate to enter on this second class of duties without emasculating itself, and dwarfing the nation whose powers it is called on to develop. The collective community, represented in its government, possesses the most royal rights; and it cannot neglect them or lay them aside without irreparable loss. It is, indeed, a mistake of great moment for the government to overshadow the citizen, to push him from his footing, and so to mar the units in its own make-up; but this fact does not alter the other fact. that there are forms of large and generous activity which devolve on the combined energy of the nation, and serve pre-eminently to develop and establish the national life. These two forces, individual life and national life, are held together and skillfully harmonized in the healthy State. In this second class of duties, too important to be overlooked, and too great or too urgent for individual strength, we would place education. The duty of education is put by those who object to any large entrance on the labor by the

State on too narrow a ground. It is said to be a measure of self-defense, not a measure of national development. This cannot be true in a republic. A government which is of the people, by the people, and for the people, can need no defense against the people. Such a government has no life which it has any wish or right to defend against those who institute it. Education is not, then, with a republic a measure of self-defense, but one of national development.

In the same narrow way a division is attempted between primary and higher education, and the first only conceded as a right to the State. It is said, the State may not tax its citizens for expenditures whose returns reach to a small portion of the population. This assertion is wrong in every bearing of it. It underrates the breadth of the advantages that accrue from higher education, and it equally underrates the rights of the State in its own up-building. Is there any more inequality of returns to the people in a university than in a light-house? in a college than in a common school, to a man without children, or to one who chooses to send his children elsewhere? Has the State no right to tax its rich citizens for the commonweal, and has it the right to marshal its poor citizens into its armies, and bid them lay down their lives for that same commonwealth? No such narrow calculation of personal gains will guide us correctly in dealing with a great public interest. The State may do what the State needs to have done, and it may put its hand on all the means and the men required for the accomplishment of its purpose.

We come, then, fairly to the second portion of our inquiry, Is edncation a duty which it is necessary for the State to take up? If it is not such a duty, it is not for one or other of two reasons. Either the importance of education is not sufficient to commend it to the State, or it is a work that may be adequately done by private citizens. I need not lose time on the first point. My text is too deeply imbedded in our convictions. Wisdom is the principal thing. Observe, also, the ways in which national wealth and national energy run to waste when this form of activity is denied them: the forts and the prisons, the navies and the armies, the wars and the tyrannies, the intrigues and jobbery which come in to drink up the national life, turned from its true channels. The nation, like the individual, must have a higher life, if the brutal one of violence and bloodshed is to be kept down; if the narrow, astute and unscrupulous impulses of commerce are to be enlarged; if the craft and cunning of men, emulous only of power, are to find correction. Indeed, the only consideration at issue among patriots is the second one, Can and will the citizen do this work of education sufficiently well?

Here arises another division of sentiment. Quite a portion of our citizens would remand all education to private effort, would commit it more especially to religious bodies, to be guided and fostered by them. A second class would sustain the primary schools as a public institution, and leave higher instruction to private munificence, to the guidance and support of the churches. We shall consider the second opinion only; not because it is the most consistent one, but because it is the most influential one, and has somewhat the force of a tradition with us. If, moreover, we show higher education to be a duty of the State, that position will carry with it primary training.

Higher education as developed by the churches is unsystematic, partial, feeble, divided. It is unsystematic. The churches are not in agreement as to the extent or methods of this work, and there is not even the appearance of consultation between them on any of these questions. Each religious body pursues its own purposes in its own way, and thus there is neither completeness nor harmony, so far as the efforts of others, or the wants of the community, are concerned. Such instruction is partial, It is too much to hope that every church will thoroughly care even for its own. Some churches have an inadequate notion of what a sufficient provisicn implies. But if the children of its own membership could be safely entrusted to each church, there remains a large number of citizens who are not attached to any faith, and to whom sectarian institutions are distasteful. These citizens are not provided for, nor are they in any condition to provide for themselves. Higher education, as controlled by churches, is feeble, often very feeble. The best of these institutions in the West not only admit this fact, they daily urge it as a reason for aid. There are very few among us who can make the large gifts necessary for the endowment af a college. The result is, that sectarian institutions in the West are inadequately supported, and are compelled to drag on in poverty, and beg funds in the East to be expended in communities too rich to need the gift, and too proud properly to acknowledge it. Sectarian colleges, feeble as they are, are unreasonably multiplied, and made, by very numbers, aggressive on each other. A Congregationalist, in love with his own institutions, forgets that he is not equally pleased with Methodist instruction; and both, urging their own claims, fail to remember that they look askance at a Lutheran school, or with aversion at a Catholic college, resting on the same basis with themselves. A Congregationalist would be likely to say ot a State university, that it is to be preferred to a Catholic college; and a Catholic would as naturally reply that a State institution has the field as opposed to heretical institutions. Thus, in a State like Wisconsin, no one person can find himself in sympathy with any considerable portion of private education, but rather ready to contend with much of it for possession of the field. The result is, that in religious education there is the same wasteful effort to pre-empt the Kingdom of Heaven which we see in our churches. A small village has three spires where it should have but one, and five where two were better.

Thus, sectarian education, notwithstanding its commendable self-denial, has shown itself, taken as a whole, in the West incomplete, uneconomical and uninfluential. An advocate partially confesses the fact, and covers it with the remark, "Looking over the numerous State institutions in our country, we believe that, taking them as a whole, they show no better educational results than those colleges that have owed their origin to the voluntary principle." So far as this statement is a reflection on State universities, it is sufficient to say, that hitherto church training has so divided public sentiment, that State institutions have not been honestly treated in their funds, heartily trusted in their instruction, or carefully watched over in their development. The public temper is changing at this point, and very memorable results, as in Michigan University, are being reached. It is not the past, not even the present, but the future which belongs to public education.

To this general objection of divided effort in the voluntary method, multiplying semi-hostile institutions, is incident the equally grave objection, that the unity of an educational system being lost, the fragment which falls to the State in common schools is left utterly unsupported. One of two results is alone possible. Either the common schools will increase in strength, conquer for themselves the grammar school, the high school, the normal school, and so open a way up to the university, the last link of the chain; or, losing hold of the public mind, they will sink into insignificance. A system of education is a living thing, and will win the field that belongs to it, or wither away. In the Eastern States this tendency of strength has been very discernable. The public schools have vanquished the academies, and taken possession of intermediate instruction. In some of the older States, universities, I doubt not, would have been organized, had not the field been adequately occupied by *quasi* public institutions, like Harvard and Yale.

On the other hand, the difficulty with which common schools, left to themselves, confront a tendency on the part of the influential classes to private instruction, is seen in the Southern States. The public school is not a power in those States; because it is so limited in its uses, and does not command the sympathy of the upper classes. If education in higher branches is wholly private, if the line of division is complete here, the attendant spirit of disintegration will work its way downward, set apart the common schools to a labor disparaged in public sentiment, and dishearten them and burden them in every effort and every argument by their inferiority. No system of education defensible in each member, and strong with a common strength, is likely to be constructed out of the jarring elements of public and private schools. The one or the other must conquer, and be made the organizing power, while the defeated element will become an incumbrance.

An equally weighty reason for maintaining public education is found in the division of our national life between nationalities, between sects, between classes; a division sure to vex and weaken us unless we systematically remove it. The hopeless anarchy of the South has its foundations here. In the West, similar forces are in full operation. Our prosperous development must depend on our ability to assimilate, in full citizenship, all nationalities, all sects, all classes. There are with us such class divisions of race, religion and social impulses, separating the community into portions relatively equal, that nothing but the most vigorous and undisturbed national life can overcome them, and build us up, one State. All other influences combined are not comparable with public instruction as a means of reduction and assimilation; and in it the continuity of discipline, from its commencement to its close, is of chief moment Churches and nationalities that fear this reconstruction, instinctively attack the public schools. If each sect and nationality is to reclaim its children as soon as possible from public instruction, to train them in its own way for its own ends, we shall baffle the constructive forces that work for us, and abolish the conditions of success. If each church, each party, shall struggle to capture the State for itself, rather than stand together on common grounds, we shall substitute weakness for strength, discord for harmony, and convulsion for progress.

This consideration of national unity may seem remote, but it is one of the last importance in these Western States. In no higher object, in no nobler work, can our various populations and diverse religious bodies be united than in this of complete, public education; and if they reject this union, they reject it in behalf of strife and dissension.

In no way can the coming generations secure such unity of feeling and strength of common footing as by one, protracted and thorough intellectual discipline. This division of our national life, this distraction of social sentiment, this waste of educational resources can be immediately reduced and ultimately removed by extended and systematic public instruction.

Guided by the experience of the East, we are constantly forgetting the changed conditions of our Western development. The Eastern States grew up slowly, with no sudden, transcendent demand for education: material growth and institutional growth were deliberate, spontaneous and concurrent. In the West, a single generation of strangers from all quarters of the globe construct a large, powerful and populous State, whose institutions must be framed at once, and put in operation.

In the East, there was, during the formative periods, comparative harmony of religious thought, and one prevailing nationality; in the Western States, more than half the population may be, as it is in Wisconsin, of foreign extraction, with a corresponding diversity of religious faith and social customs. In the East, there were a harmony and concentration of educational forces unknown to us. Harvard was built up conjointly under public and private action, with no diversity of feeling. Yale, in the same way, for a long time expressed the strength of a colony and of a State. In other institutions, as in Princeton, there has been a concurrence of effort not again possible. The last exceptional concentration of religious energy in a college, is that which founded Oberlin. Private effort in the West has shown haste, division and weakness. In the East, there is much accumulated capital and a spirit of systematic benevolence; in the West, wealth is diffused, there is commercial pressure everywhere, and the passion for money-making burns unabated.

It is not, therefore, the true policy of the West, with its abundant yet scattered resources, to rely for education on an ambling, halting voluntaryism, but to lay hold of its own wealth by taxation, and to build for its motley population common and sufficient institutions, in which the young life of the State can be at once and vigorously shaped, and so a new era ushered in. It is the duty of the West to rear her institutions, not with narrow jealousy between sect and sect, section and section, but on her own broad foundations, with large-hearted emulation, and so to become a stately column of strength in the social development of the new world. For these Western States to divest themselves of their grand prerogatives, and beg at the hands of their own citizens or elsewhere what they only can adequately do for themselves, is to cripple and dishonor the public life.

Education has also somewhat changed its character in the progress of years. Instruction in the physical sciences has taken new forms, and assumed new importance. But this instruction demands expensive appliances, and hence large endowments. The feebler institutions of the West, previously unable to compete with the prestige of Eastern colleges, can do it under these new conditions with still greater difficulty. To leave our youth dependent on poorly endowed colleges, is to consign the most ambitious of them to the East for education, to still further depress our home training, and affix to it a permanent stigma of inferiority. There is but one institution in the West, Michigan University, that really competes in public patronage with the older Eastern colleges. Michigan has shown us the only way in which a truly commanding university can be built up among us.

We have been speaking simply of two methods of education, and of their respective value. Nothing, therefore, that we have said is to be construed into disparagement of particular institutions. The weakest sectarian colleges have some value, and the best great value. Instruction of a high order and of the best spirit is often given in them. We only regret that in so many instances it is poorly supported by surrounding conditions, and does not rest on a foundation from which it can reach the entire community.

We believe that experience fully confirms the view now taken. When the States west of New York began to be settled, the voluntary principle was in the ascendant. Not till recently has the opposite opinion gained much favor, and it still only divides public sentiment. State universities, up to the present time, owe their strength chiefly to the general government. They have rarely received honest, to say nothing of liberal, treatment from the States themselves. This feeling is changing and to change, but their present condition is not a just presentation of the system. Yet the educational power of the West is largely in them, and passing over with each year to them. One great success has been achieved. Other universities are encouraged by it, and are pressing forward into the same rank. As these institutions shall gain ground, they will justify themselves by their efficiency, economy and commanding power. Let us look at a few facts which point to this result. The colleges of

Ohio have been founded under the conviction that higher education is to be entrusted to voluntary effort. She is a wealthy, powerful State, with every advantage of position, and a relatively homogeneous and educated population. What is the result of the voluntary principle operating under these favorable conditions without check? She has nine universities and thirty-three classical colleges. Of these forty-two institutions scarcely one can be said to have a national reputation, and the most of them are not known beyond their own immediate vicinity. Harvard alone exerts far more general influence than they all combined. The educational strength of Ohio in higher departments, notwithstanding her excellent public schools, is subdivided to the last degree of weakness. Her own influence barely passes her borders, while her sons wander East and West in search of an education that imparts stimulus and carries power. Yet these forty-two institutions occupy the time of three hnndred and twenty-five instructors, and, while nearly all are miserably poor, they conjointly consume a magnificent revenue.

A college can hardly justify its permanent existence that has not one hundred and fifty students. The necessary initial outlays, and the time of a full corps of professors, are not paid for in public advantage by such a college, while its students, if well taught, lose the incalculable gains of large associations, and the sense of surrounding power. No man can be educated by feeble contact, any more than he can be guided by a glow-worm.

Yet the colleges of the United States average only seventy-four students, a mark far below the minimum of admissibility. Herein is a sad squandering of labor and reduction of educational values. Concentration, accumulation, vigor are our first demand. We have frittered away our time, our resources, and our national life, by the petty and divided efforts of sects and localities.

Look at the result of the opposite policy as now being developed in Michigan. She has one university and nine colleges. The university contains about the same number of young men as do the colleges conjointly, and commands an influence and concentrates an educational energy compared with which the power of any one of these institutions is insignificant. Yet, by the census of seventy, the income of the university is given as less than that of the colleges, while her professors number only one-half theirs. A similar result is being rapidly reached in this State.

Many elements, indeed, enter in to modify comparisons of this sort, and make them illusory. The University of Michigan contains a large per cent. of professional students, and the nine colleges add to these young men half as many more young women. On the other hand, the grade of scholarship in some of these colleges will bear no comparison with that of the University, and many of their students are in preparatory work. We cannot, however, be mistaken in the primary fact, that the educational power of Michigan finds grand expression in her university, and there only.

While many of the advantages now claimed for public instruction would be admitted by its more candid opponents, there are two very grave objections urged against it. These difficulties are real, are not to be denied or evaded, but are to be met and overcome in a manly spirit. The first of them, and to my mind the greatest of them, is the inability to secure a large-minded, firm and frugal administration of public instruction. It is the form of that pervasive difficulty which belongs to all our national action, and, indeed, to human progress. Yet it is the struggle with this danger and like dangers that brings to life its noblest duties and rewards; it is a victory over this difficulty and like difficulties which constitutes the best triumphs of the constructive force of human society. If we give ground for such a reason as this, we shall deserve the stinging reproach, "A people inferior to their institutions."

We are not to lose time in regretting such obstacles. We are to meet them again and again, till success crowns our efforts. It may easily happen, it does happen, in every grade of instruction, that those to whom the interests of education are committed are ready to say, Here is power, here is honor, let us enter into them; and so they forget the single high end they should pursue. The time will come, and public education will hasten it, in which educational men will gather influence within their own field, and become the servants of the State to counsel action as well as to carry it out. To conciliate and affiliate the best educational and the best political sentiment in the one work of public education is a victory of constructive order second in value only to the object to be accomplished by it. Educational, like judicial, action, demands and will secure a sacred enclosure of public sentiment, which will put it beyond the invasion of private interests.

A second objection more persistently urged is, that the subject-matter of higher education requires a discussion of moral questions, and questions that have a religious bearing, and that these discussions cannot be entered on freely, fairly and fully in a public institution; and that no sufficient religious safe-guards can be thrown about young men in a State university. This, also, we look upon, not as one of those obstacles which simply block the way, and do nothing to repay the labor of removal, but as one of those supreme moral conflicts in which it is the very purpose of our lives to overcome, their only proper nobility. We admit the danger, we see the difficulty, we address ourselves to it as wise and faithful men, and we fully believe that a most complete and incomparably valuable success is possible to us. We would have good men and able men, earnest men and men of various tendencies and views, as our instructors, and then we would give them freedom; and our young men and young women, just passing into manhood and womanhood, freedom under them, and, on the whole, with the constant and careful correction and recorrection of experience, we have no fear of the results. It is a bigoted and unworthy claim that nothing which has a religious bearing shall be discussed in a public institution, a claim of the same narrow character as the claim that certain convictions, and those only, should be enforced in a college. Either method is one of fear and bondage. Many things stated on many sides by many good men, nothing urged beyond the conviction which earnest thought always bears with it, this is our method, a method safer and better, we believe, than instruction that is narrowed down to a single dogmatic system, and enforced on all sides as an authoritative belief. We would stand, in the completion of our educational work, as God puts us, on the great plains of truth, and on its high mountains, in contact with many things, and gathering instruction and impulse from them all. If we build up our faith as a castle, and set up our doctrines as its gates, and gather in whom we can as camp-followers, and leave the many to shift for themselves, we run the silent, subtle risk, which has been the crowning risk in the world's history hitherto, that of narrowing dogma, stifled sympathy, interior corruption and slow decay. Nothing is safe; the nearest approach to safety is the honest effort to make all things safe on common grounds of advantage, and this means public instruction.

With all cordiality, then, toward all good instruction everywhere, we still feel that a public system commends itself to these Western States by the immediateness, sufficiency and economy of its action; by the harmony under it, and consequent strength, of all departments of education; by the unity of the national life which it expresses and nourishes; by the increased breadth of popular thought which it promotes; by the enlarged and patriotic impulses which it calls forth, crowding back narrow incentives, and assigning the nation its true position; and by the wise, patient spirit with which it overcomes administrative difficulties, and unites all interests in one large and liberal work.

Members of the Graduating Class:

You may not fully accept what has now been said, but whether you do or do not, having taken at the hands of the public a great gift, you are doubly pledged to the action of intelligent, patriotic citizens. The State has educated you for yourselves and for it. The two things are not in conflict, but they can only be harmonized by a noble life. To such a life, at least in its social bearings, you are pre-eminently bound. You have no right to seek your own weal, if your own weal doos not include the public weal. Chicanery and fraud with you will bear the further stigma of ingratitude and treachery.

It may be, however, that you assent fully to the value we have attached to public instruction. If so, your faith should not be a dead letter. See clearly the dangers of such a system, and the aid it calls for, and courageously confront those dangers, and cheerfully bring that aid. Inscribe on your banners, God save the commonwealth, and remember that his first salvation is always wisdom, wisdom. I trust to see many strong workmen, and in the foreground among them you, building patiently, intelligently and generously our public institutions, and, as chief over them all, our educational institutions.

So will you redeem your lives. As men and women you can only redeem your lives by making them parts of a larger and better life. The human soul is grafted on to the race in the love of the race; on to God in the love of

God, and so shares their immortality. As the years pass, the University will be presenting its justifications, making up its treasures of work, may your names come distinctly out in that list of the wise and faithful who have been given to the world by public instruction in the State of Wisconsin.

www.ingramcontent.com/pod-product-compliance
Lightning Source LLC
LaVergne TN
LVHW020635110826
845149LV00004B/1198
* 9 7 8 1 4 1 8 1 9 1 1 8 4 *